Adventures at Camp Pootie-Cho

Good Manners ABCs
Activity Book

Ophelia S. Lewis

**Character illustrations by
Shabamukama Osbert**

VILLAGE TALES PUBLISHING

Copyright © 2019 Ophelia S. Lewis

All rights reserved. Copying, printing and distribution of this book without permission is a theft of the author's intellectual property. No part of this publication may be reproduced without prior written permission of the copyright owner.

The age when a child is ready to begin using coloring books varies from child to child. The pages of this book are suitable for crayons and color pencils.

A catalog record for this book is available from the Library of Congress

LCCN: 2019912909

ISBN: 9781945408540

First published in the United States in 2019

By Village Tales Publishing

Lawrenceville, GA 30043

Interior & Cover Designed by OASS

Character illustrations by Shabamukama Osbert

Printed in the United States of America

This book belongs to:

_____

Liberia

The setting for Camp Pootie-Cho is Sapo National Park, located in Sinoe County, Liberia. In 2018, Village Tales Publishing began publishing The Adventures at Camp Pootie-Cho series using native animals living in Sapo National Park as characters. These adventures take readers into the tropical Liberian rainforest to learn from its special animal campers.

Sapo National Park is the country's largest protected reserve. Many endangered animals inhabit the park, which represents one of the most intact forest ecosystems in the region. The park covers about 697 square miles of rainforest that is home to many special animals; including forest elephants, pygmy hippos, chimpanzees, antelopes and many other wildlife. Named after the local Sapo or Sao tribe, it was formed in 1977 under the Division of Wildlife and National Parks. Mr. Alexander Peal was in charge.

Join us on our adventures at Camp Pootie-Cho!
www.camppootiecho.com

Meet Camp Pootie-Cho campers. Throughout the book, the campers will help you learn your Good Manners ABCs. Learn the American Sign Language alphabets and numbers too.

Sapo Potamus (Pygmy Hippo)

Gola Potamus (Pygmy Hippo)

Bendu Cuma (Zebra Duiker)

Quama Elphan (Elephant)

Quincy Elphan (Elephant)

Cyrus Shepherd (Lamb)

Faaz Chimp (Chimpanzee)

Asatu Chimp (Chimpanzee)

Riah Peppers (Pepper Bird)

Solo Dawg
(Mixed-breed Dog)

Lazzie Croc
(Dwarf Crocodile)

Kweeta Giraffy
(Giraffe)

Jenks Monkie
(Monkey)

Nawei Patherson
(Black Panther)

Razaq Lyons
(Lion)

Meet Camp Pootie-Cho hard-working staff.

Mr. Drill Bayogar
Camp Director (Drill)

Rev. Ida Shepherd
Pastor (Sheep)

Nurse Cuma
(Zebra Duiker)

Meet Camp Pootie-Cho staff.

Officer Yeahum
Security Guard (Warthog)

Sekou Pupoh
Sports Director (Goat)

Oldman Juuku
Grounds Keeper
(Diana Monkey)

Dr. Viola Harris (Duiker)
Guidance Counselor

Mr. Gaimuni
handyman (Pangolin)

Dogs, goats, giraffes, and sheep are not native animals living in Sapo National Park, but they are part of the popular animals living in Liberia.

Mr. Daffeh
Bus Driver (tree frog)

Chef Chewie
(African leopard)

Ms. Una Clawson
Administrator (Bee-eater)

American Sign Language Alphabets
ASL is expressed by movements of the hands and face.

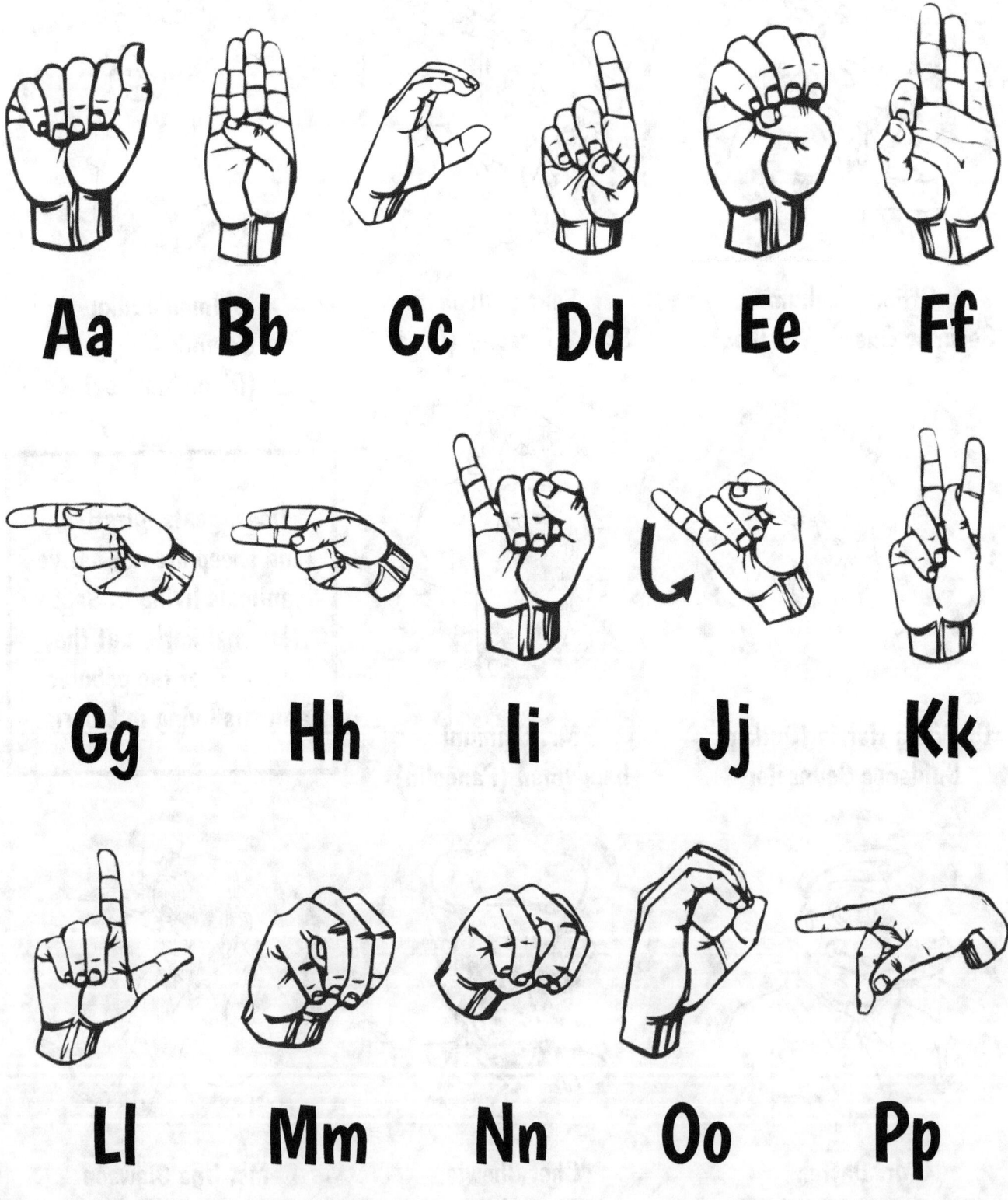

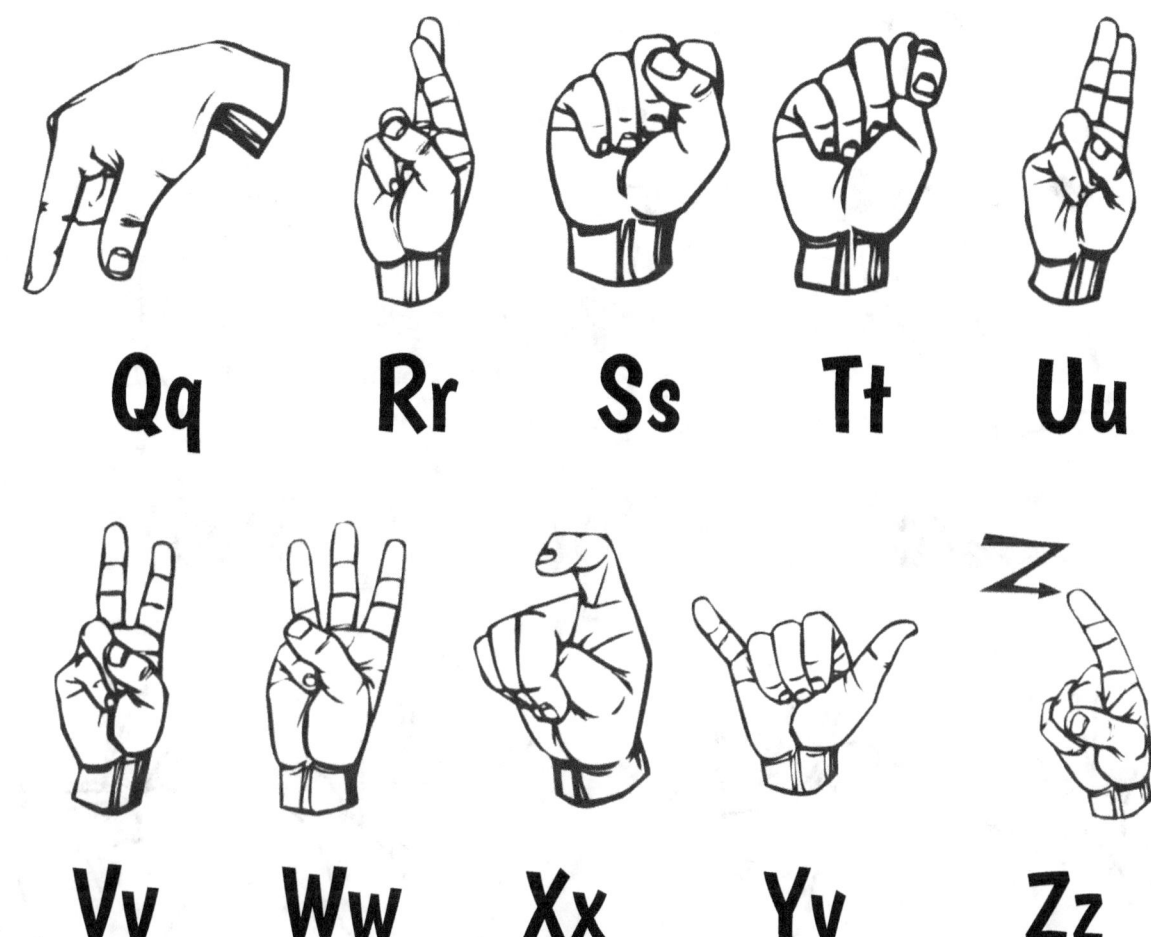

What is Faaz's message?

Faaz is speech impaired and hearing impaired. He cannot speak or hear, so he communicates with his hands using the ASL.

American Sign Language Numbers

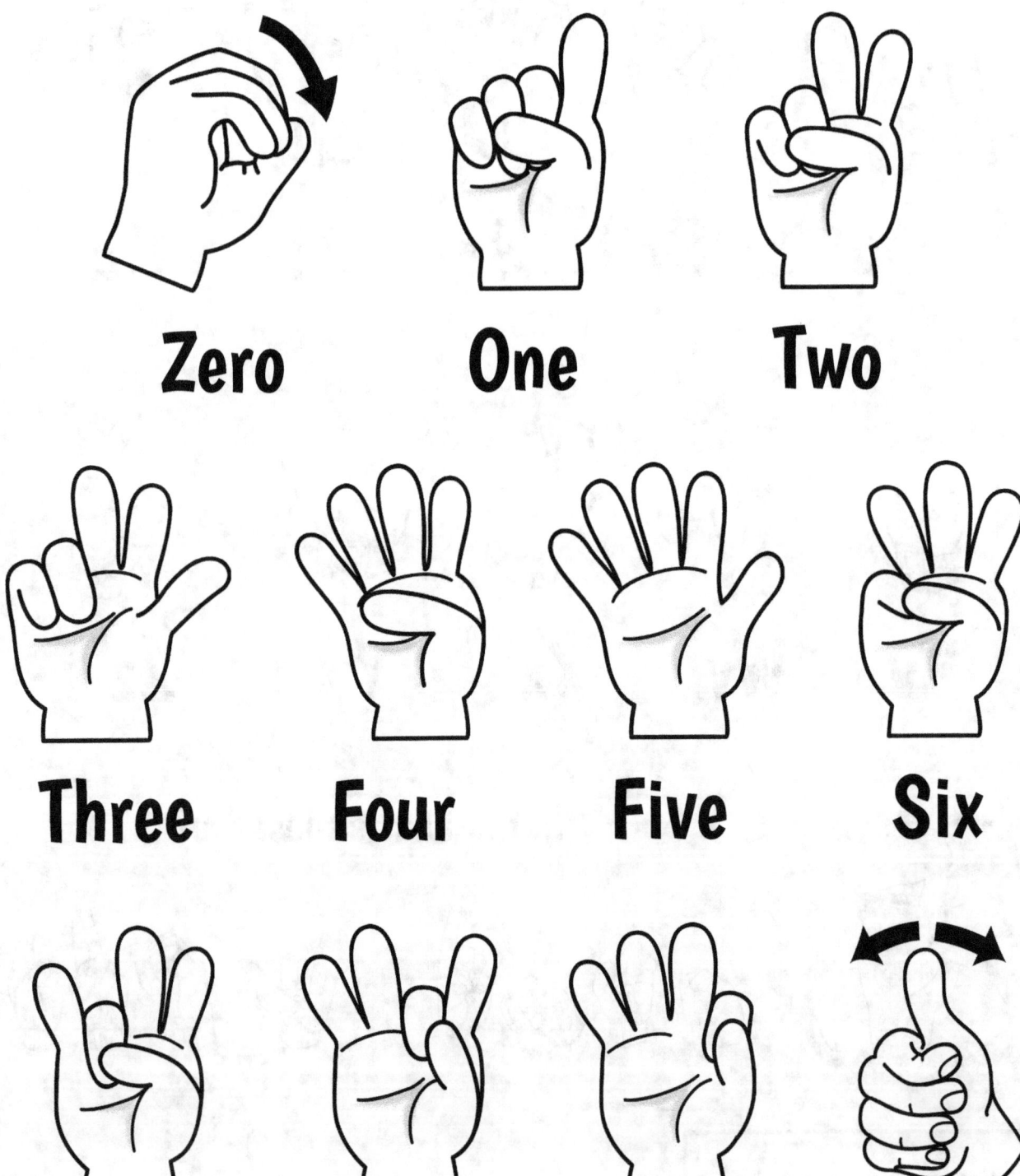

Respectful boys and girls
always practice polite habits
when they are at home, at school,
at the playground, and while sitting at
the table too. Consideration for others is
a good way to start.

You must learn good manners to be
thoughtful, kind, and smart.
Are you a Super Polite Kid?

No worries. To be a super polite kid,
it's as easy as the ABCs.
Learn, and then remember,
to follow these simple one-liner rules.
You will get a certificate too!

Aa

Aostelda signs A.

Arrive on time.

Try not to be late.
Being on time matters.
It tells people you respect them.
It's important to be on time.

Help Asatu find her clock.
She likes being on time.

BENDU CUMA

My name is, Bendu. It's good to have patience. We don't have control over something like the weather, but we can have control over our attitude. You don't have to be gloomy. You don't have to be upset over something you don't have control over. Be patient.

balloon

Cc

Ciatta signs C.

Close doors quietly.

Jump at a chance to help someone.
Open the doors for others. Also hold doors for others.
Do not slam doors, your little brother or sister
could get hurt if they are with you.
Close car doors and house doors quietly.

candy

hot chocolate

Use your indoors voice
when you are in the house,
or in class, or at church.

cookies

CYRUS SHEPHERD

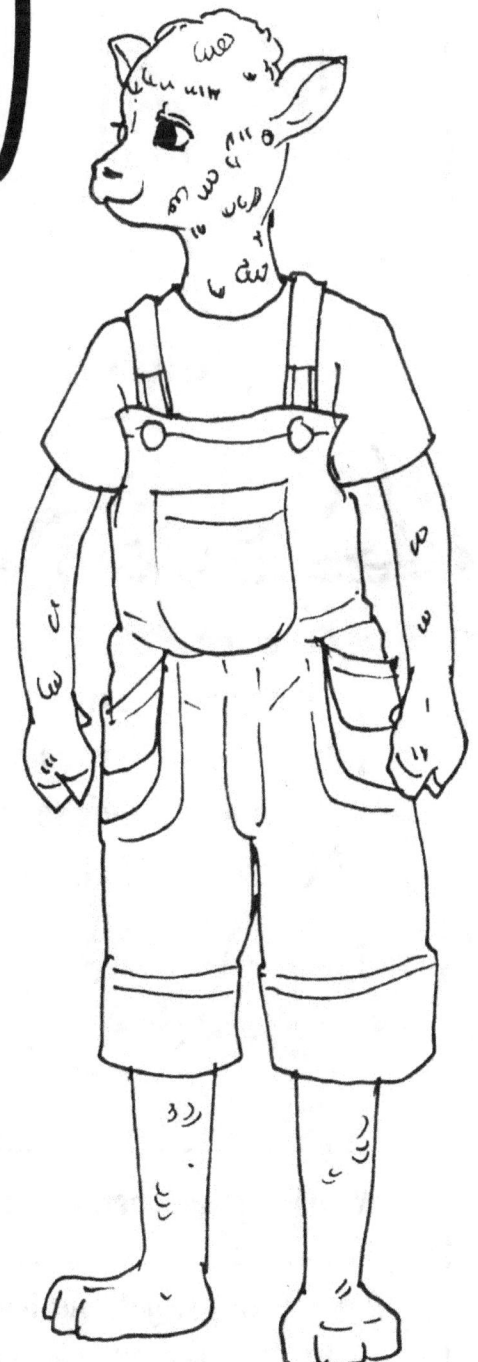

> Hi, my name is Cyrus. I'm a lamb. I was adopted. Rev. Shepherd is my Mommie. Use your indoors voice when you are in the house. I'm quiet in church. I use my indoor voice.

Search-for-Words

Places where we have to be quiet.

LIBRARY	SCHOOL	FUNERAL
CHURCH	CINEMA	HOSPITAL
		MUSEUM

```
P V N K N A Z Z N
B H F C M R Y N C
F K O E H R H S B
M U N S A U C B M
L I N R P H R U R
C C B E O I S C G
G I K O R E T G H
L F L K U A L A F
N P N M T G L L L
```

Dd

Des signs D.

duck

Don't pout.

When Mr. Daffeh asks campers to fasten their seatbelt, and they pout, he tells them, "Don't pout." Everyone has to follow the rules. It is rude to pout. Polite boys and girls don't pout.

dress

Connect the dots

We don't always get what we want. Sometimes you get mad. Sometimes you are sad. Don't pout when you are sad or mad. The best way to get your feelings out is to calm down. It's not polite to scream and shout either. Count, one, two, three....

MR. DAFFEH

My name is, Mr. Daffeh. I am the bus driver at Camp Pootie-Cho. I'm responsible for the safety of all campers and staff riding the bus. I make sure everyone is using their seatbelts.

19

Ee

glass

Elijah signs E.

fork

Elbows off table.

Sit up straight at the table and keep your hands on your lap. Do not hunch. Keep your elbows off the table.

Mind your table manners.

spoon

- Wash your hands.
- Sit up straight, do not hunch.
- Don't be a messy eater.
- Use spoon or fork to eat most foods.

- Do not talk with food in your mouth.
- Chew with your mouth closed.
- Use a napkin to wipe food off

QUINCY ELPHAN

> My name is, Quincy. I'm Quama's little brother. People expect you to have good manners if you want to spend time around them.
> It is important to practice having good manners so you can know how to act when around others.

your face or hands.
- Use your napkin in your lap to help catch any spills or crumbs.
- Do not burp or fart when eating with others.
- If you do, say "Excuse me".
- If you cannot reach something, ask nicely for it to be passed to you.
- Do not make slurping sounds or other noises.
- Do not play with food or smash it around.

Ff

Farah signs F.

Finders can't be keepers.

Why can't you keep what you find?
Keeping what belongs to someone else is stealing.
Look for the owner of what you find and give it back.

frogs

FAAZ CHIMP

Hi, my name is Faaz.
I am a chimpazee.
I'm deaf. I am not able to hear or speak. I sign with my hands and make facial expressions to tell people what I want to say to them.
I can sing, laugh, and make jokes like everybody else.
I can spell too.

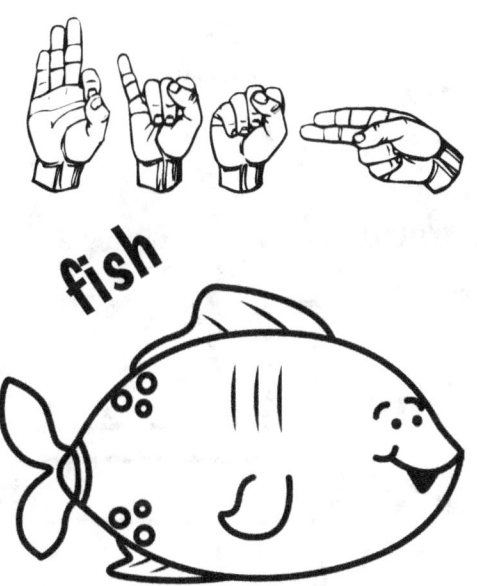

fish

Gg

Gboto signs G.

Go to bed without fussing.

Thirty minutes is good for afternoon naps.
Go to bed without fussing.

Good-night, its bedtime.

Gogo is ready for bed.

GOLA POTAMUS

Hi, I'm Gola. I'm a pygmy hippo, Sapo's little sister. I hate to take naps.

pillow

This is Gogo, my favorite toy.

Hh

Hadoo signs H.

Hand stuff over. Don't throw.

Throwing things might get friends hurt.
Hand stuff over. Don't throw.

Hands can do many fun things.

- clap your hands,
- play patty-cake,
- hold a balloon string,
- tie your shoelaces,
- wave good-bye,
- hold things,
- sing a song in sign language,
- squeeze a small ball,

SAPO POTAMUS

Sapo is a Pygmy Hippo. His family is from Sinoe County, Liberia. He likes to make friends and explore hiking trails through Sapo National Park.

Hands can do many fun things. Hands are not for hitting.

- fingerpaint,
- pick a flower,
- write a note,
- pet a dog or cat,
- play the air guitar,
- hold hands with someone,
- show off your yo-yo skills,
- greet someone with a handshake,
- give yourself a pat on the back.

Ii

Ian signs I.

iguana

Interrupting is not nice.
Sit quietly and listen when someone is speaking.
No one is heard when everyone talk at once.
Here's a really good advice; interrupting is not nice.

REV. IDA SHEPHERD

> I am Rev. Shepherd. I tell the campers that God is always willing to forgive naughty boys and girls, but I put them in timeout.

- it is rude to interrupt.

- What to do if you need to talk to someone who is already busy talking. Wait patiently until they are done talking. Politely ask or tell them what you wanted to say. Then, they will listen to you.

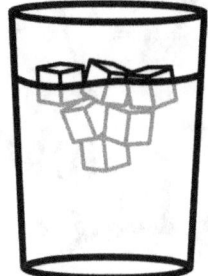 ice

 ice cream

29

happy

Jeanos signs J.

Remember, everyone has feelings.

Jokes shouldn't hurt others.

A laugh is a blast for pranks and gags.
Chuckles are good for bloopers.
But, jokes shouldn't hurt others.

sad

mad

Draw three character emotions.

JENKS MONKIE

> I'm Jenks. I'm a monkey and I love sports. I'm always playing and joking around with my friends, but I try not to hurt their feelings. Jokes should make people laugh, not hurt their feelings.

Jenks' Jokes

Joke: Why was 6 afraid of 7?

Joke: What did the little corn say to the mama corn?

Joke: Where would you find an elephant?

Joke: What did the banana say to the dog?

Joke: What kind of tree fits in your hand?

Kk

Kaela signs K.

key

Knock and wait to hear, "Come in."

When you want to go inside a room when the door is closed, knock and wait to hear, "Come in". Then open the door.

Personal Space

It is important to respect other people's personal space. People do not like it when you get in their personal space. You have to ask before you touch someone else.

KWEETA GIRAFFY

Find your personal space. Using a hula hoop, hold it around your waist; that is likely your personal space bubble. When people get closer than that, and it makes you feel crowded and uncomfortable, politely say, "You are in my personal space. Please move back a little."

Hey, I'm Kweeta. Get to know your personal space. Do not allow everyone into your personal space. Look at the circle and know who you share your personal space with.

Personal Space

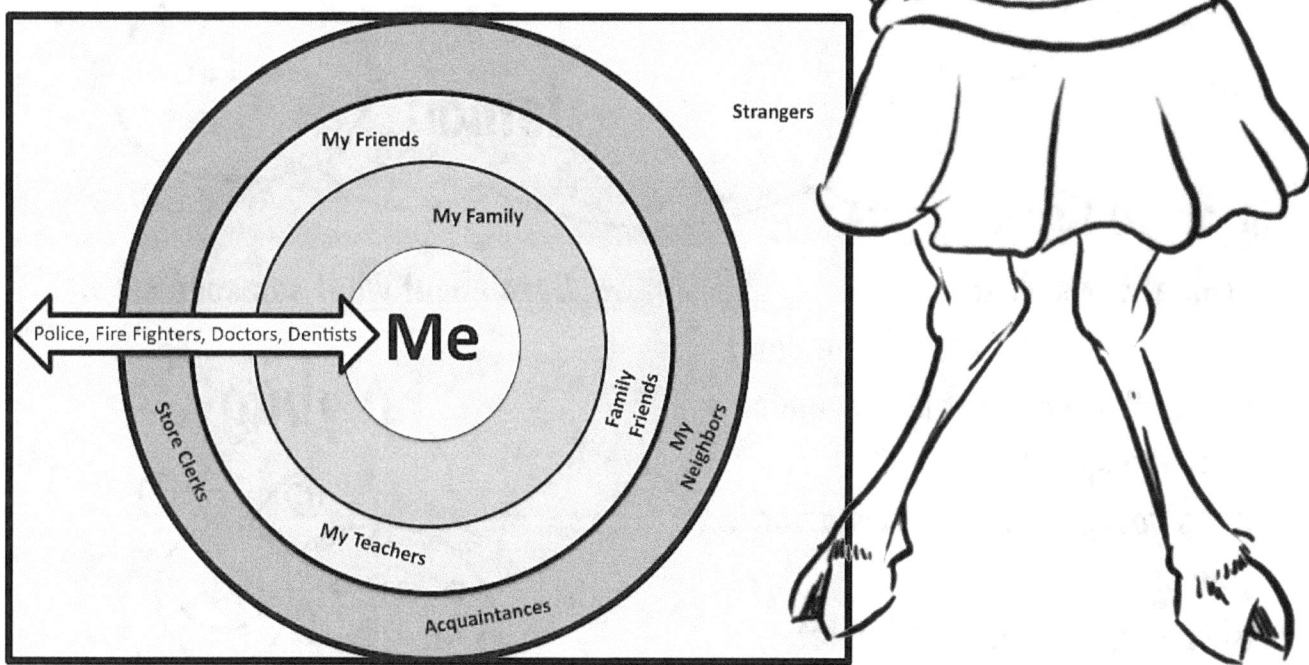

Ll

Lem signs L.

llama

Listen closely.

When someone is talking, it's good to hear new ideas. Listen closely so you can understand what they are saying.

lemon

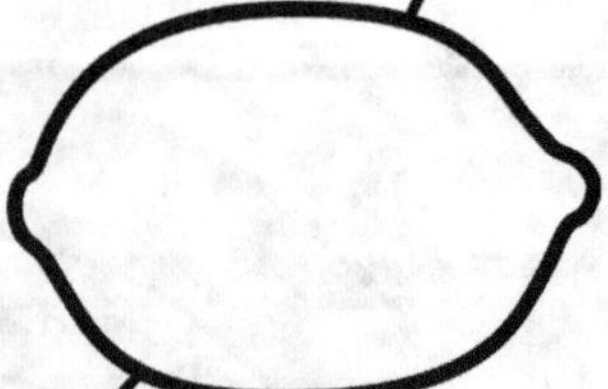

How to listen.
- Look at the speaker.
- Keep your mouth closed and don't talk with others or make sounds.
- Face the speaker.
- Keep your hands at your side or in your lap.
- Keep your feet still and quiet.
- Care about what someone says.

ladybug

LAZZIE CROC

laptop

It's good to think about someone else's idea. I like to hear new ideas when people are talkiing. I listen closely so I can understand what they are saying. Sometimes I learn something new.

lamp

lemonade

Manny signs M.

moon

mat

"May I?"
is a good way to ask.

When you want something that someone has, do not demand. "May I?" is a good way to ask.

money

mail

mouse

NAWEI PANTHERSON

Search-for-M-Words

I'm Nawei. I'm a Black Panther. Sometimes I like to play by myself. Sometimes I like to play with my friends. May I be your friend?

muffin

mailbox

Nette signs N.

No hats at the table, please.

Boys and men should take off their hats
when they enter a house
or when they sit at the table.

More table rules for everybody.
Wash your hands before coming to the table.
Do not sit with your elbows on the table.
Do not talk or drink with food in your mouth. Do not be greedy.

NURSE CUMA

> I'm Nurse Cuma. I take good care of sick or injured campers and staffs. I mind my bedside manners.

Things at the clinic.

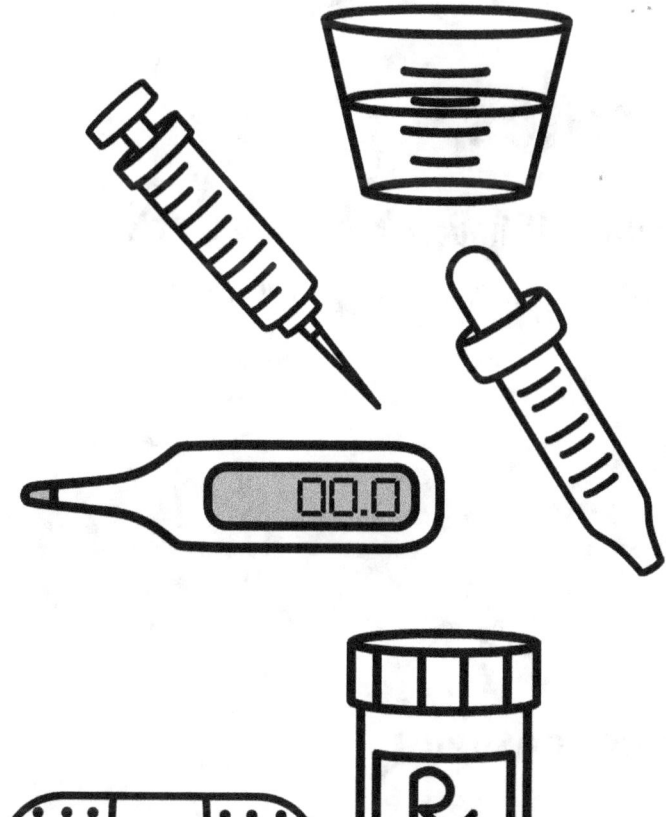

Oo

Ophie signs O.

owl

Obey rules.

Following directions is important.
First you must listen, pay attentation, and obey the rules.

Basic Rules to Obey

Keep your neighborhood clean.
Do not throw trash on the ground.
Put banana peels, crumbled paper and other trash in the trash can.

OLDMAN JUUKU

People call me, Oldman Juuku. I keep the camp clean. I'm responsible to cut the grass, clear fallen trees and clear paths through the woods. I make sure all the signs are clear so people can follow directions and obey the rules.

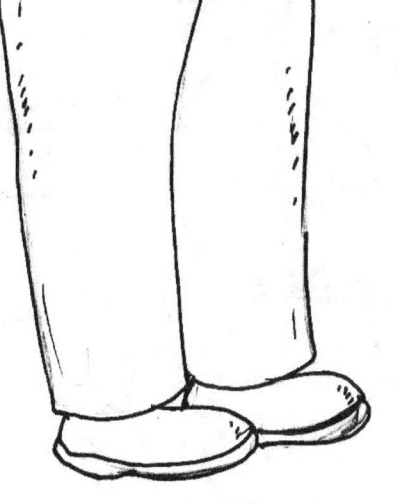

Pat signs P.

potato

Pay attention.
Stop. Look. Listen.
Especially when you are crossing a street.
When someone is talking, focus and look at the speaker.

pill

pencil

pepper

panda

42

Queeta signs Q.

Quit wanting to be first all the time.

Don't be a sore loser either. Don't get mad and stop playing.
You will make the game less fun.
Try really hard to keep playing even if you are losing.
You can avoid fights by letting someone else go first.

QUAMA ELPHAN

"Hey, I'm Quama. I am a Forest Elephant. Ask me anything and I'll probably know the answer. I'm not always the first to answer questions even if I know the answer."

Overcome the need to always be first.

Rr

Razaq signs R.

rabbit

rice ruler

Role-model kindness to others.

Do not bully. Do not cheat.
Do your best when you compete.
To be proud of your work, you must give your best efforts.
It's okay to make mistakes. Do not give up.
You can always try again.

road rat rocket rhino

MR. GIAMUNI

"I am a Pangolin, an ant eater. Everybody calls me Mr. Giamuni because that's my name. I build things around Camp Pootie-Cho. I also fix things. Best of all, I am a good role-model to the campers and staffs. I treat everyone with respect. I always show kindness."

Search-for-R-Words

```
G T R U L E R R
R R O C K E T X
R V I R N R N W
G H O C A K X H
T A I B E K Z C
D Y B N N K N N
D I M B O R R T
T T L V R A T R
```

Sydni signs S.

seal

Share your toys.

Be a good playmate. Be a good friend.
Let others play along. Do not be selfish.
Share your good toys too.
How would you feel if no one share with you?

shirt

star

snake

smelly shoe

SOLOMON DAWG

My name is Solo. It's short for Solomon. I'm the best player on my basketball team. I'm a good playmate. I look out for teammates and let others play along.

sun

Search-for-S-Words

S	M	E	L	L	Y
B	H	K	N	E	S
S	G	I	K	Y	T
D	U	A	R	R	A
K	N	N	J	T	R
S	R	S	H	O	E

49

Taipee signs T.

table

"Thank you" and "Please" are good courtesies.

Never be rude to anyone, whether older or younger than you. Remember to say "Thank you" or "Please" ; "Yes, Sir" or "Yes, Ma'am" or "No, Sir" or "No, Ma'am."

turtle

taxi

truck

CHEF CHEWIE

"I'm Chef Chewie, I make all the goodies at Camp Pootie-Cho. The campers thank me when I serve them food. They also say, "Please," when they want a cookie or a drink."

tiger

Search-for-T-Words

T	T	A	X	I	R
U	R	I	N	R	M
R	N	H	G	D	J
T	H	V	K	E	N
L	G	Z	T	G	R
E	T	R	U	C	K

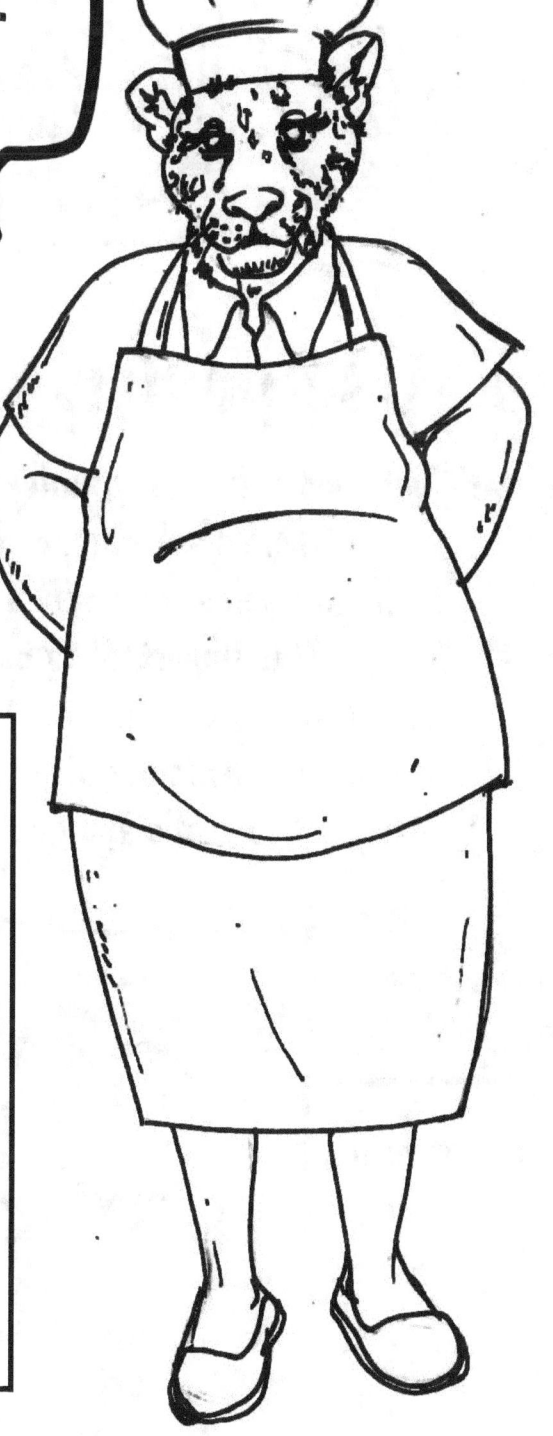

Ulysses signs U.

Use positive words.

It's not good to be bossy, unless you are the boss.
There's a difference between
reminding someone kindly and being bossy.
It is important to be polite.
Use gentle words and a gentle tone of voice.
Do not cuss. It is not nice to tease or fuss.
Use positive words and give a compliment.

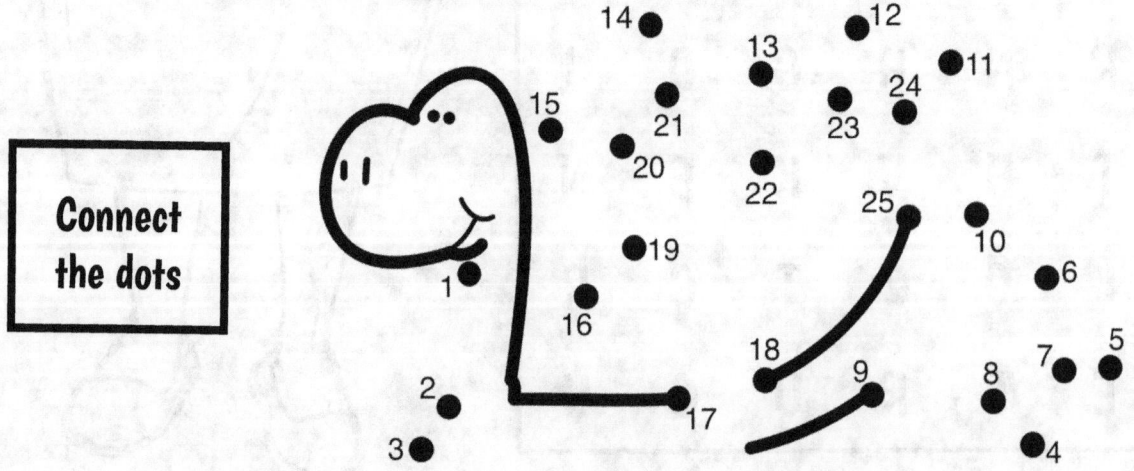

Connect the dots

MS. UNA CLAWSON

My daily office job is to organize, and arrange all meetings. I take care of emails, bookkeeping, and answer the phone. I always smile or say something nice.

Connect the dots

Vv

Vero signs V.

Views of others must be handled tenderly.
A new student or a new neighbor might be from a different country.
Or might talk differently and wear different clothes.
Don't make fun of them or call them names.
Get to know someone new. Invite someone new to play.
Introduce yourself. Make a new friend.

van

vest

vet

54

DR. VIOLA HARRIS

I'm Dr. Harris. I have a passion for working with children. I am happy to help the campers learn good manners. I teach them how to treat other people that look different. People are all different and special. They do different things. Different families may look different too. It's always good to respect those who look different from you. Views of others must be handled tenderly.

Search-for-V-Words

```
R V A N F R D
R R A K W R R T
T M F T T S R
C P V C E Q T
L I Z V P E M
Q R M K V Q G
W E V F X X Y
```

55

Ww

Wokie signs W.

weasel
2 Across

web
2 Down

Wait your turn.

It is fair to take turns.
You play with something a little,
and your friend plays with it a little.
Do not jump ahead. It's good to help someone.
Look out for playmates too.

whale
1 Down

worm
1 Across

COACH PUPOH

I'm Coach Pupoh. I referee all the games and make sure there's fair play. Be patient and wait your turn.

Write in the Letter W Crosswords

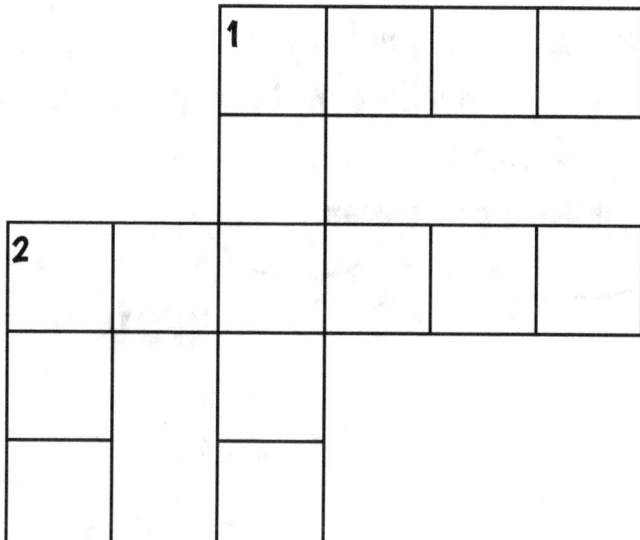
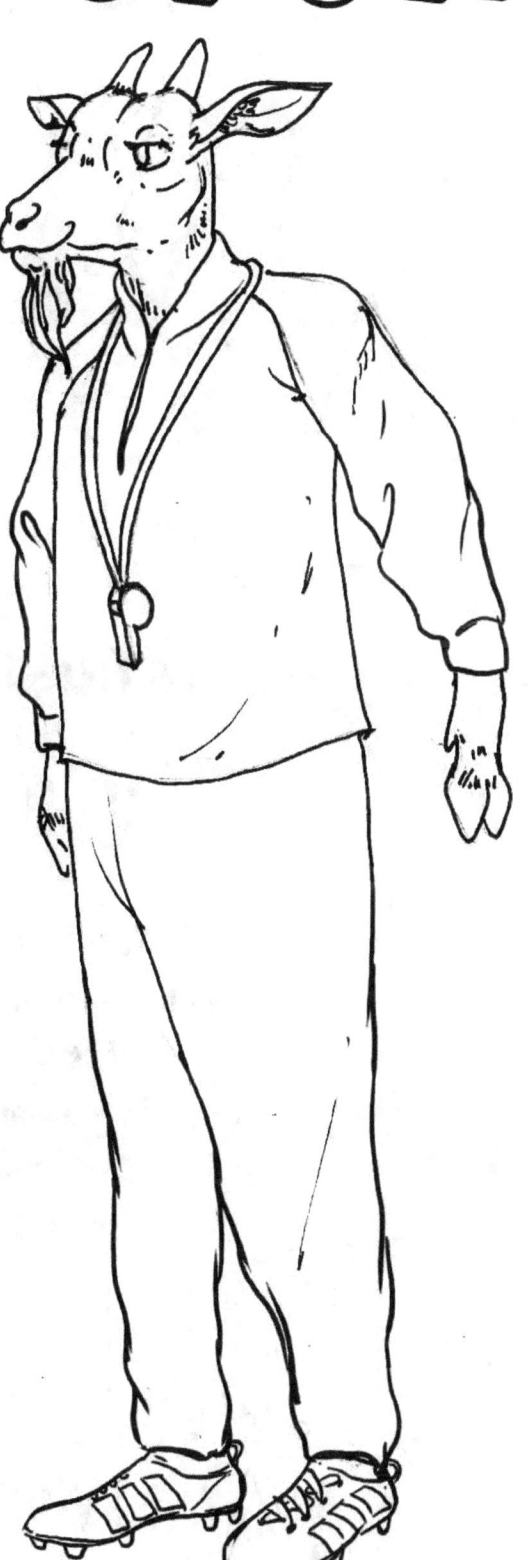

Xx

Xena signs X.

xantus
1 Across

"eXcuse me, please," is a key phase.
It's always good to say, "eXcuse me, please," when you burp, or if you fart, or if someone is standing in the way. It is also a good time to say it if you want someone's attention.

xylophone
2 Across

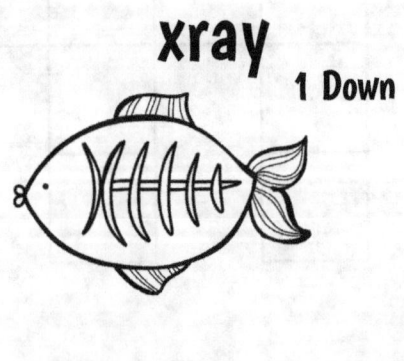

xray
1 Down

Mr. Drill Bayogar is the boss. He loves being in charge, and nothing bugs him!

MR. BAYOGAR

Respect Authority

Respect anyone who is in charge, even the babysitter. Just because she isn't your Mom doesn't mean you don't have to respect her. Your Mom put her in charge so she has the authority to tell you what to do and you have to listen.

Write the Letter X Crosswords

Yekee signs Y.

yarn

"Yes" sounds better than "Yep" or "Yeah"

Answer politely when your name is called. "Yes" is a positive word. It needs to be heard.

yam

yacht

yogurt

OFFICER YEAHMU

"I'm Officer Yeahmu. I patrol the camp and make sure everyone is safe. Every night I call roll to make sure everyone is present and safe."

Search-for-Y-Words

```
Y T K Q Y C
O Y Y L T Y
G V A A V A
U Y J C R M
R L A L H N
T L V K K T
```

Zz

Zyra signs Z.

Zooming is for outdoors.
Playtime is fun time.
Do not play ball in the house.
We have fun playing active games outside,
so should you.

zero
3 Across

zebra
1 Down

zoo
2 Down

Write in the Letter Z Crosswords

62

ZAQ LYONS

> My name is Razaq, my friends call me, Zaq. I'm a lion. I play on the third-grade football and basketball team. Zippy is how you feel when you work to get along with those around you. They will like you and you will like you.

zipper

2 Across

63

Mind your manners at School & the Library

- During story time do not talk to another person, listen to the storyteller.
- Be careful with videos, books, and computers in the library.
- Use your inside voice in the library and in class.
- Return library books on time.
- Read silently to yourself in the library.
- Say "please" when you ask for help.
- Show respect for teachers and classmates.
- Share your colored pencils with a friend.
- Do not talk while the teacher is talking.
- Clean up after art class.
- Stand in line quietly before recess.

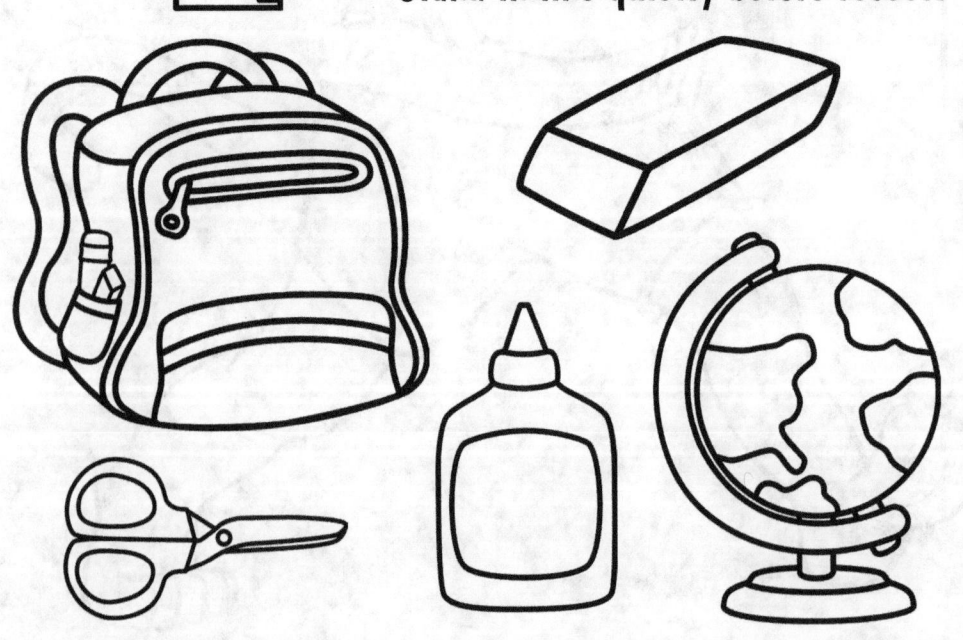

QUIET PLEASE! TEACHING AND LEARNING IN PROGRESS

Mind your manners on the Playground

We love recess every day.
We go outdoors to play, play, play.

Help others.
Follow the rules.

Be patient.
Wait your turn.
Make new friends.

Be safe and have fun.
Keep hands to yourself.
Take turns and share the equipment.
Look out for playmates too.

Mind your Table Manners

- Make sure your hands are clean before eating.
- Sit still in your chair during mealtime.
- Take small bites of your food and keep your mouth closed while chewing.
- Smacking or slurping your food or drink is rude.
- Chew your food before you talk.
- Use a napkin when you have food on your face.
- Ask to be excused if you want to leave the table.

Things you SHOULD NOT do while sitting at the table:
- Don't speak with your mouth full.
- Don't use your fingers to eat.
- No tipping or spilling food. Don't make a mess.
- Don't throw food. Don't kick under the table.

Congratulations!
You've earned your
Super Polite Kid certificate!
Remember to be patient and kind,
and show respect towards others.
Most of all, show love.

A mission to transform the limited books available with African characters in children's books today, drawing from her own childhood for inspiration, Lewis creates cultural-genre books with African characters all children can relate to. Of her work, she says, "The best way of getting people familiar with the importance of identity and own surroundings is through the eyes of childhood. Start at the earliest stage of life." Learn more about her work at www.ophelialewis.com

Ophelia S. Lewis
Author

Shabamukama Osbert

Illustrator

Since joining Village Tales Publishing in 2016, Osbert has done illustrations for several books by different authors; BALLAH MAKES SHAPES (Augustus Y. Voahn), TOBY PANNOH'S GOOD MANNERS FOR BOYS AND GIRLS and KEEPING SECRETS (Ophelia S. Lewis), LITTLE BRAVE LYDIA and DRAMA ON PIPELINE ROAD (Nemen M. Kpahn), and BETTER TOGETHER (L.M. Logan)

Puzzles Answers

Page 9 Faaz's Message
Mind Your Manners.

Page 13 Find Asatu's clock

Page 14 Bendu's book

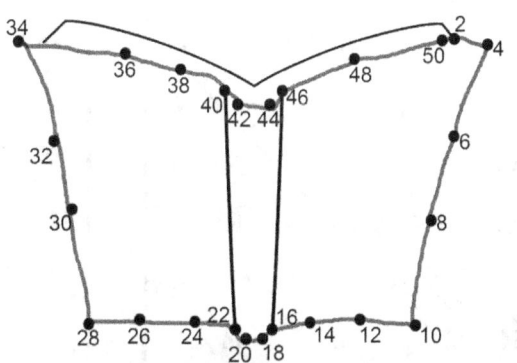

Page 17 - Places to be quiet.

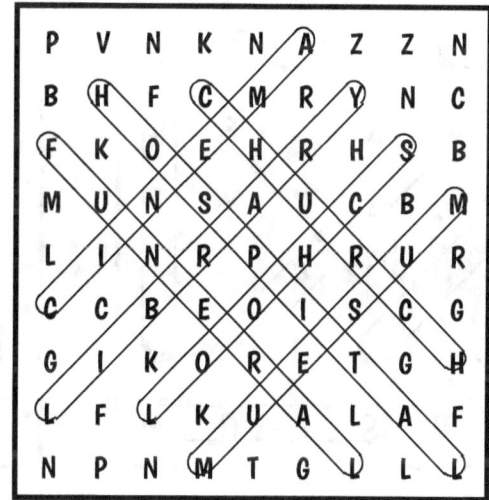

Page 19 Mr. Daffeh's poodle

Page 31 Jenks' Jokes

Joke: Why was 6 afraid of 7?
Ans: Because 7, 8, 9

Joke: What did the little corn say to the mama corn?
Ans: Where is pop corn?

Joke: Where would you find an elephant?
Ans: The same place you lost her!

Joke: What did the banana say to the dog?
Ans: Nothing. Bananas can't talk.

Joke: What kind of tree fits in your hand?
Ans: A palm tree!

Page 37 Search for M words

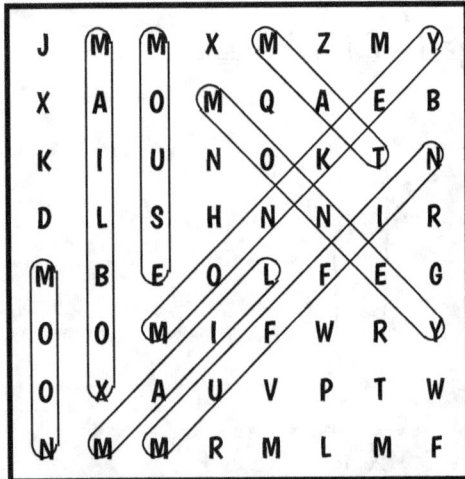

Page 47 Search for R words

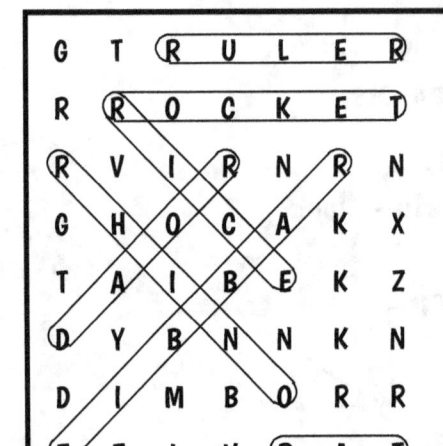

Page 49 Search for S words

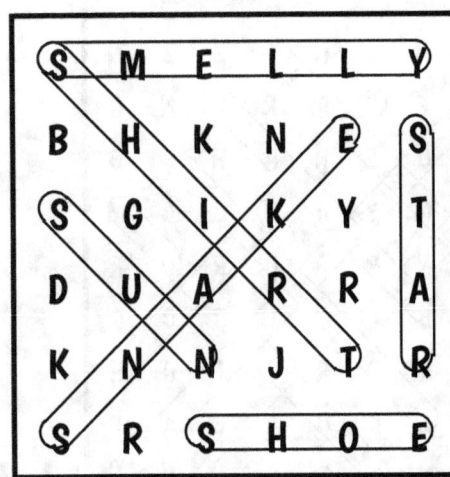

Page 51 Search for T words

Page 52 Connect the dots

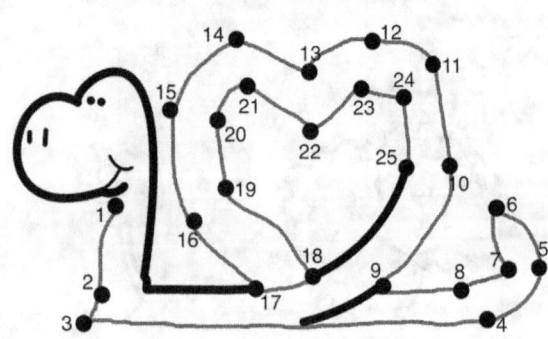

Page 53 Connect the dots

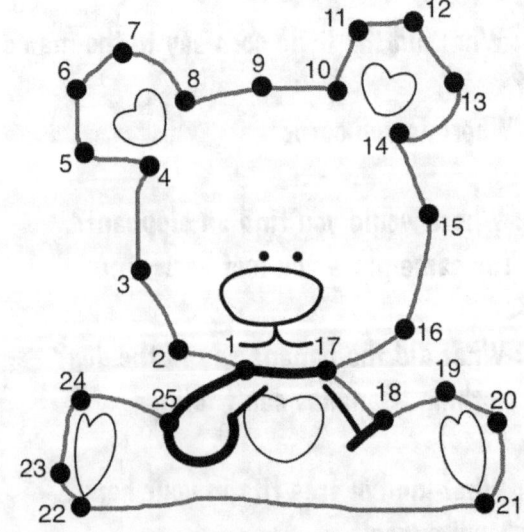

70

Page 55 Search for V words

Page 57 Letter W Crossword

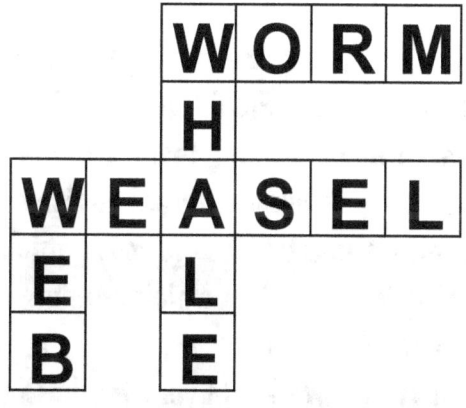

Page 59 Letter X Crossword

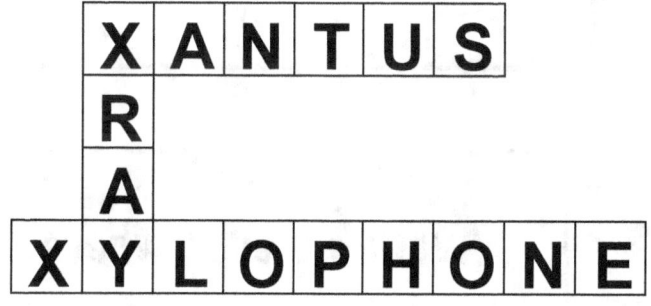

Page 61 Search for Y words

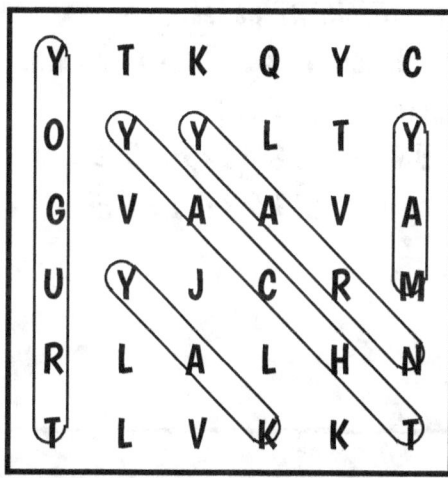

Page 62 Letter Z Crossword

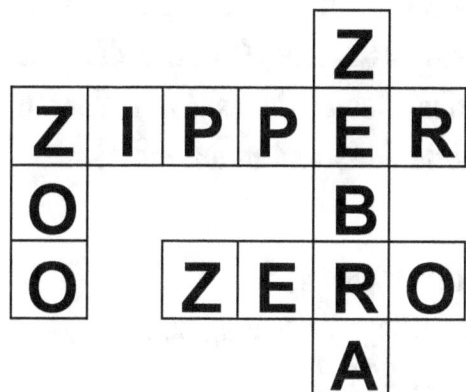

Join us on our adventures at Camp Pootie-Cho!

Learn more at www.camppootiecho.com

Follow us @camp_pootiecho

Our first book, Better Together: in this adventure, it's Field Day. Solo Dawg and Zaq Lyons become team captains. As they race through different obstacles, the campers must choose to move quickly or stick together. See which animals make it and which ones don't, in this fun story about teamwork. On your mark. Get set. Go!

Paperback: 27 pages
Publisher: Village Tales Publishing (October 3, 2018)
ISBN-13: 978-1945408335
Dimensions: 8.5 x 0.1 x 8.5

Available everywhere books are sold.

Dozens of challenging fun games and puzzles from the Adventures at Camp Pootie-Cho. Try your hand at Mazes, Crosswords, Coloring Activities, Secret Codes, Word Search, Sudokus, and much more!

Paperback: 119 pages
Publisher: Village Tales Publishing (October 15, 2018)
ISBN-13: 978-1945408397
Dimensions: 8.5 x 0.3 x 11 inches

www.ingramcontent.com/pod-product-compliance
Lightning Source LLC
Chambersburg PA
CBHW080022130526
44591CB00036B/2577